FOOTBALL
THE QUIZ BOOK

knowledge // quizzes // puzzles

CREATED **BY FANS** FOR FANS

Other books in this series

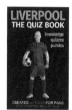 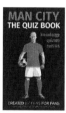 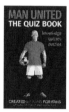 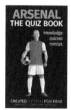 

Publisher Information

Published by **Created by Fans for Fans**

Copyright © 2019 Created by Fans for Fans

Contents

FOOTBALL
THE QUIZ BOOK

knowledge // quizzes // puzzles

WHO AM I #1?

#1 I was born in Tuscany, on the 28 January 1978.

#2 I began my career with Parma.

#3 I won the Golden Glove at the 2006 World Cup.

#4 I have played more than 175 internationals for my country.

Who am I? _____

ANSWER AT THE BOTTOM OF THE NEXT PAGE

ON THE MAP:
European Cup Winners

As of 2019, twenty-two teams had won the Champions League or European Cup. One point for each team, and another point for every one you can place correctly on the map below.

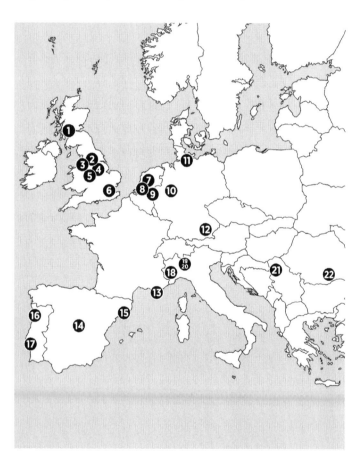

#1 _____   #12 _____

#2 _____   #13 _____

#3 _____   #14 _____

#4 _____   #15 _____

#5 _____   #16 _____

#6 _____   #17 _____

#7 _____   #18 _____

#8 _____   #19 _____

#9 _____   #20 _____

#10 _____   #21 _____

#11 _____   #22 _____

ANSWERS ON PAGE 56

QUIZ 1:
Early Doors

#1 Who said, "I'm going to make a prediction - it could go either way"?
John Motson or Ron Atkinson?

#2 Who was the top scorer at the 2014 World Cup finals?
Thomas Muller, Karim Banzema or James Rodriguez?

#3 Who won the first FA Cup Final in 1872?
Royal Engineers, Wanderers, or Old Etonians?

#4 Which goalkeeper has played over 150 times in the Champions League?

#5 Marta is considered one of the best female footballers of all time. Which country did she play for?

#6 The English Football League Cup has had many names over the years, but which of these names is made up?
Rumbelows Cup, Worthington Cup, or Nationwide Cup?

#7 Who was the top scorer in the very first Premier League season?
Teddy Sheringham, Andy Cole, or Alan Shearer?

#8 Which team did Luis Suarez play for before Liverpool?

#9 When were goalkeepers first allowed in football?
1861, 1871 or 1881?

#10 In which country do the team Newell's Old Boys play?

ANSWERS ON PAGE 53

NAME THE TEAM:
England World Cup 2018 Semi-Finalists

We've given you the initials of the team that played Croatia in the semi-final of the World Cup. Write down the full names on the page opposite.

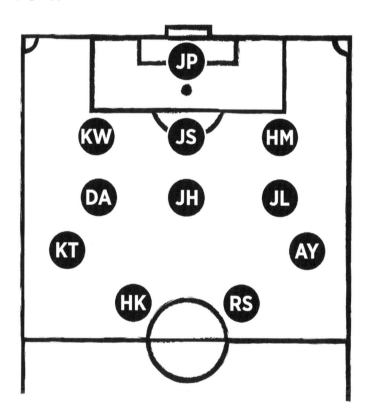

#1   **JP**   _____

#2   **KW**   _____

#3   **JS**   _____

#4   **HM**   _____

#5   **DA**   _____

#6   **JH**   _____

#7   **JL**   _____

#8   **KT**   _____

#9   **AY**   _____

#10   **HK**   _____

#11   **RS**   _____

ANSWERS ON PAGE 68

MISSING LETTERS:
Players

#1   _ A _ _ _   _ A _ E

#2   I _ _ A Ï _ A   _ A _ _

#3   _ E _ I _   _ E   _ _ U _ _ E

#4   _ I _ _ O _   _ I _ _ E _ Ö _

#5   _ A _ _ U _   _ I _ _ O _

#6   _ I _ _ A E _   _ E A _ E

#7   _ O _ _   _ A _ _ _ E _

#8   _ E _ _ _   _ E _ O

#9   _ A _ I O   _ A _ É

#10   _ Ï _ A _ _ O   _ E _ E Ï _ A

ANSWERS ON PAGE 64

WORD SEARCH #1:
Find the Top Premier League Scorers

```
J  A  V  A  N  P  E  R  S  I  E  Q  M  J  Z
M  O  D  Y  U  F  D  P  K  N  H  A  G  R  R
M  Q  N  R  O  Q  X  J  D  Y  H  A  S  E  F
F  M  A  N  B  C  W  C  T  G  F  N  B  R  F
U  V  N  E  L  Y  L  V  N  L  S  E  C  A  D
E  S  I  H  R  V  D  I  Q  A  Y  W  P  E  A
Q  V  D  F  D  X  R  R  I  Z  Z  O  C  H  F
B  H  R  Z  X  E  E  R  A  S  Y  I  O  S  J
A  Q  E  N  H  F  O  O  I  P  F  A  Z  F  O
Z  O  F  S  G  P  F  O  K  M  M  T  R  H
E  V  T  G  X  Y  E  N  O  H  F  A  E  Y  E
Y  N  E  L  O  C  D  E  W  W  N  U  L  M  G
N  C  A  U  S  L  Z  Y  L  T  G  K  F  S  Z
L  I  J  K  Y  B  Q  T  E  A  V  X  R  T  F
X  S  J  V  P  W  I  W  R  K  K  Q  D  W  Q
```

Cole, Kane, Owen, Defoe, Henry, Aguero, Fowler, Rooney,
Lampard, Shearer, Ferdinand, VanPersie, Sheringham

ANSWERS ON PAGE 59

9

ANAGRAMS:
English League Grounds

#1   Big Mod Drafters   _____

#2   Country Dig   _____

#3   Die Like Muskrats   _____

#4   Dismays At Strum   _____

#5   Doors A Poking   _____

#6   Fine Lad   _____

#7   Hi Flutist Dogma   _____

#8   Loaned Lard   _____

#9   Mu Ex Lion   _____

#10   No Stupid Wigmaker   _____

ANSWERS ON PAGE 67

QUIZ 2:
Over the Moon

#1 Who said, "If we played like this every week, we wouldn't be so inconsistent"?
Paul Gascoigne or Bryan Robson?

#2 Which two teams played in the 1974 World Cup Final, and for a bonus what was the score?

#3 Which of these grounds has the FA Cup Final NOT been played at?
Kennington Oval, Anfield or Old Trafford?

#4 Which country's teams have won the European Cup/Champions League the most times?

#5 Who won the first women's Ballon d'Or?
Carly Lloyd, Lucy Bronze or Ada Hegerberg?

#6 Who won the very first EFL Cup?
Birmingham City, Aston Villa, or Chelsea?

#7 Eleven of the first twelve Premier League titles were shared between Man United and Arsenal. Who won the other one?

#8 Which country does Robert Lewandowski represent at international level?

#9 In what year was the back-pass rule introduced? 1992, 1994 or 1995?

#10 In which country do Club Necaxa play?

ANSWERS ON PAGE 57

BEAT THE CLOCK:
The Start of the Premier League

You have five minutes – can you name all the teams that played in the very first Premier League season (1992/3)?

#1 _____   #12 _____

#2 _____   #13 _____

#3 _____   #14 _____

#4 _____   #15 _____

#5 _____   #16 _____

#6 _____   #17 _____

#7 _____   #18 _____

#8 _____   #19 _____

#9 _____   #20 _____

#10 _____   #21 _____

#11 _____   #22 _____

ANSWERS ON PAGE 55

MATCH UP:
Match the Player with the Country

#1	Alireza Jahanbakhsh		Scotland
#2	Seamus Coleman		Ireland
#3	Sead Kolasinac		France
#4	Michael Hector		Iran
#5	Joel Matip		Cote d'Ivoire
#6	Granit Xhaka		Spain
#7	Andrew Robertson		Cameroon
#8	Nicolas Pépé		Bosnia-Herzegovina
#9	Rodri		Jamaica
#10	N'Golo Kanté		Switzerland

ANSWERS ON PAGE 91

QUIZ 3:
Park the Bus

#1 Which country won the very first World Cup?

#2 Who were the first Welsh team to win the FA Cup?

#3 During the 1970s two teams won the European Cup
three years in a row. Can you name them?

#4 Which World Cup winner scored 49 goals in EFL Cup
games?
Geoff Hurst, Bobby Charlton or Martin Peters?

#5 Who said, "Not to win is guttering"?
Andy Carroll or Mark Noble?

#6 Pele only played for two club teams during his career. One was Santos in Brazil. Can you name the other?

#7 What does VAR stand for?

#8 In which country do the team Hadjuk Split play?

#9 In 2015 John Carver managed which Premier League club for twenty games?

#10 Who said, "If history repeats itself, I should think we can expect the same thing again"?
Kevin Keegan or Terry Venables?

ANSWERS ON PAGE 61

WHO AM I #2?

#1 I was born on Valentine's Day, 1992, in Middelfart.

#2 I made my senior debut at Ajax.

#3 In January 2018, I scored a goal against Man United just 11 seconds after kickoff.

#4 I come from the same country as the actors Viggo Mortensen and Mads Mikkelsen.

Who am I? _____

ANSWER AT THE BOTTOM OF THE NEXT PAGE

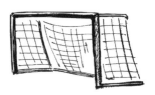

MISSING LETTERS:
English League Teams

#1   I _ _ _ I _ _ _ O _ _

#2   _ _ A _ _ _ O O _

#3   _ _ A _ _ O _ _ _ I _ _

#4   _ A _ _ O _ _

#5   _ _ E _ _ E A

#6   _ I _ _ O _ _ E _ _ E _ _ O _ _

#7   _ E I _ E _ _ E _ _ I _ _

#8   _ _ I _ _ O _ _ I _ _

#9   _ _ E _ _ O _ _ O _ _ _ E _ _

#10   A _ _ E _ A _

ANSWERS ON PAGE 63

WORD SEARCH #2:
Players

```
K  J  W  Y  H  T  A  N  W  T  F  E  K  W  H
O  N  Z  R  P  Q  P  G  F  M  O  B  Q  H  R
O  S  C  X  I  O  A  E  I  B  S  E  U  X  I
N  E  U  P  T  S  H  P  K  X  F  Q  D  R  F
A  F  I  M  A  S  T  O  R  R  E  I  R  A  W
G  W  E  Y  M  P  I  C  K  F  O  R  D  U  T
O  Z  Y  A  N  D  E  R  S  O  N  B  A  R  G
D  E  D  L  E  R  I  E  W  R  E  D  L  A  V
N  R  A  P  O  A  J  E  T  R  U  D  P  Z  U
U  I  S  H  A  Q  Z  X  Z  L  T  V  Q  S  P
G  U  J  R  A  T  O  L  S  G  S  T  N  V  H
N  G  F  M  H  Z  O  W  G  K  N  L  F  E  E
W  A  E  B  V  P  V  J  R  U  G  N  H  P  F
W  M  B  X  C  U  K  Y  O  B  Y  D  N  F  Z
U  Q  L  Z  V  P  W  M  Z  Q  S  P  L  J  V
```

ZAHA, MATIP, MOUNT, MAGUIRE, ANDERSON, GUNDOGAN, PICKFORD, TORREIRA, ALDERWEIRELD

ANSWERS ON PAGE 69

NAME THE OPPOSITION:
FA Cup Finals

Below are the winners of four FA Cup finals, the scores, and the scorers from the winning team. Can you name the losing team?

Arsenal
2 v 1
Sánchez 4
Ramsey 79

_____

Portsmouth
1 v 0
Kanu 37

_____

Wigan Athletic
1 v 0
Watson 90+1

_____

Wimbledon
1 v 0
Sanchez 37

_____

ANSWERS ON PAGE 80

QUIZ 4:
A Game of Two Halves

#1 Italy won their first World title in 1934. Where was the match played, Rome or Paris?

#2 Which team has won the European Cup more times than they've won their own domestic league?

#3 Who said, "The first ninety minutes of a football match are the most important"?
Pep Guardiola or Bobby Robson?

#4 England's women reached the semi-finals in both the 2015 and 2019 World Cups. Which teams knocked them out?

#5 Who were the first team to be relegated from the Premier League twice?
Crystal Palace, Middlesbrough, or Nottingham Forest?

#6 Maradona's international career ended in the middle of the 1994 World Cup finals. What was the reason?

#7 Which was formed first, FIFA or UEFA?

#8 Al Ahly are by far the most successful football team in which country?

#9 Which Portuguese club did José Mourinho first manage?

#10 Who said, "Germany are a very difficult team to play...they had 11 internationals out there today"? Neil Lennon or Steve Lomas?

ANSWERS ON PAGE 65

MATCH UP:
Where did they make their debuts?

#1	Nathan Aké	Benfica B
#2	Joelinton	Darlington
#3	Felipe Anderson	Sporting Lisbon B
#4	Dele Alli	Santos
#5	Bernardo Silva	Coventry City
#6	James Maddison	Sport Recife
#7	Rúben Neves	Chelsea
#8	Alisson	Internacional
#9	Eric Dier	MK Dons
#10	Jordan Pickford	Porto

ANSWERS ON PAGE 79

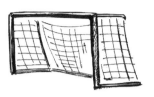

WORD SEARCH #3:
Grounds

```
J H G U O R O B S L L I H H J
J Z C R A V E N C O T T A G E
M U K R A P S E M A J T S S G
S N R O H T W A H E H T Y J P
X J V X H T U Q K G R E Z U U
K O T Q Q A S R A H L B K H N
E Z T O P Q A X L L O F F I V
L Z U G U P F V A O V L O N M
W P W D A C B V D V P T M M F
B S L L J N E X J I D E N Z S
J L L H X H X D M T H O V L K
K I F W T X K R A P E D I R P
V L Y P W I E D I S R E V I R
D E N A L L L A M A R B T R L
X V D A O R S U T F O L Z W O
```

St James Park, Bramall Lane, Villa Park, The Valley, Hillsborough, Riverside, Pride Park, The Hawthorns, Craven Cottage, Loftus Road

ANSWERS ON PAGE 71

CRYPTOGRAMS:
Premier League Players

Can you work out which letters correspond to which numbers, and find the names of four footballers who play in, or have played in the Premier League recently? Start by guessing some of the common letters, or even better, try to guess a full name.

A	B	C	D	E	F	G	H	I	J	K	L	M
9							12					17

N	O	P	Q	R	S	T	U	V	W	X	Y	Z
8		21										

  __ __ __ __ __   __ __ __ A
  15 5 26 1 26   2 26 16 9

__ __ __ __ __ __ __ __   __ A H A
10 5 20 18 25 5 13 15   22 9 12 9

  M A __ __ N   M __ __ N __
 17 9 7 26 8   17 26 19 8 16

  __ __ __ __   M A __ __ P
  2 26 13 20   17 9 16 5 21

ANSWERS ON PAGE 84

NAME THE TEAM:
Arsenal 2003/4 - The Invincibles

We've given you the initials of eleven of Arsenal's Invincibles, who went the whole 2003/4 season unbeaten. These eleven players made the most appearances in the league. Write down their full names on the page opposite.

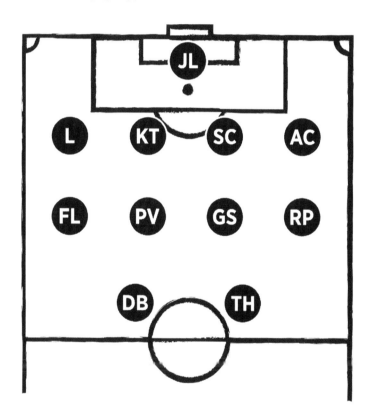

#1 **JL** _____

#2 **L** _____

#3 **KT** _____

#4 **SC** _____

#5 **AC** _____

#6 **FL** _____

#7 **PV** _____

#8 **GS** _____

#9 **RP** _____

#10 **DB** _____

#11 **TH** _____

ANSWERS ON PAGE 78

WORD SEARCH #4:
Teams

```
N  S  U  N  D  E  R  L  A  N  D  T  Z  D  M
W  Z  L  P  O  X  I  X  N  R  H  P  U  E  A
M  A  S  T  O  N  V  I  L  L  A  T  B  T  N
N  I  O  H  Y  O  T  N  U  Y  L  W  A  I  C
O  Y  D  Y  Y  T  I  C  E  K  O  T  S  N  H
T  E  T  D  U  M  X  T  I  X  O  E  X  U  E
H  M  C  N  L  G  J  P  Y  R  P  F  S  E  S
G  K  G  H  U  E  R  E  V  L  R  S  Q  L  T
I  K  P  R  I  O  S  T  L  U  E  R  E  T  E
R  C  P  S  J  A  C  B  C  L  V  H  M  S  R
B  B  F  E  D  G  Y  Y  R  O  I  N  F  A  C
G  S  B  V  S  K  R  C  B  O  L  Z  J  C  I
K  T  U  L  F  K  Y  H  A  R  U  I  I  W  T
C  U  Q  O  O  V  V  S  C  U  E  G  G  E  Y
P  A  N  W  H  B  F  S  T  H  R  D  H  N  C
```

Wolves, Newcastle United, Stoke City, Aston Villa, Middlesbrough, Sunderland, Derby County, Manchester City, Liverpool, Brighton

ANSWERS ON PAGE 76

NAME THE OPPOSITION:
England Games

Below are the scores in four important England internationals. Can you name the opposition?

_____ **1 v 5** **England**

Owen 12, 48, 65
Gerrard 45+4
Heskey 73'

_____ **2 v 3** **England**

Sterling 1, 38
Rashford 30

England **2 v 2** _____

Shearer 9
Owen 16

England **3 v 2** _____

Platt 25
Lineker 83 (pen.), 105 (pen.)

ANSWERS ON PAGE 74

QUIZ 5:
A Six Pointer

#1 In 2016 Derby County beat Carlisle United after a monumental penalty shootout. How many penalties were taken?
26, 29, or 32?

#2 England beat West Germany in the 1966 World Cup. Geoff Hurst famously scored a hat-trick, but who scored England's other goal?

#3 Man City scored six goals against Watford in the 2019 FA Cup Final. Which team had previously scored six in a final?

#4 Celtic reached the final of the 1970 European Cup, but what was unusual about their second round tie with Benfica in that year's competition?

#5 Between 2016 and 2019, this French team won the Women's Champions League every season. Can you name that club?

#6 Which team won the final First Division title, prior to the start of the Premier League?

#7 Who said, "We must have had 99 per cent of the match. It was the other three per cent that cost us"? Gianluca Vialli or Ruud Gullit?

#8 Man United and Man City famously tied on points in the 2011/12 season, with Man City winning the title on goal difference. How many points did they tie on?

#9 Between 2008 and 2017, Messi and Ronaldo were the only winners of the Ballon D'or. Can you name the Brazilian who won in 2007, and the player who ended their dominance in 2018?

#10 Which of these teams has Sam Allardyce not managed? Sunderland, Everton, Portsmouth, or Blackburn Rovers?

ANSWERS ON PAGE 72

BEAT THE CLOCK:
All the Uniteds and Cities

Can you name all the teams with United or City in their name?
There were 27 when we wrote this book. You've got 5 minutes!

_____

_____

_____

_____

_____

_____

_____

_____

_____

_____

_____

_____

_____

ANSWERS ON PAGE 77

WHO AM I #3?

#1 I was born in Barcelona on the 2nd February 1987.

#2 I made my Premier League debut in 2006 against West Ham United.

#3 I have taken part in successful Champions League campaigns with more than one club.

#4 I have a World Cup winner's medal.

who am I? _____

ANSWER AT THE BOTTOM OF THE NEXT PAGE

ANAGRAMS:
English League Teams

#1 A HEM UNTWISTED _____

#2 TWINS NOD NOW _____

#3 A INTERESTED MUNCH _____

#4 HOP TO THE TANTRUMS _____

#5 HONEST FORMATTING _____

#6 APT LOVER _____

#7 TEN OVER _____

#8 OUT PHANTOMS _____

#9 RAVENS CORK BLURB _____

#10 I DELUDE NEST _____

Answers on page 60

Who Am I #3? Gerard Piqué

QUIZ 6:
Give it 110%

#1 Who said, "He dribbles a lot and the opposition don't like it - you can see it all over their faces"?
Kevin Keegan or Ron Atkinson?

#2 Roger Milla was 42 when he played in the 1994 World Cup finals. Which country did he play for?

#3 Ashley Cole won the FA Cup more times than any other player. How many winners' medals does he have?

#4 Liverpool came from three down at half time to beat which team in the 2005 Champions League final?

#5 In the 2004/5 Premier League season, the team which were bottom at Christmas managed to avoid relegation on the final day. Which club performed this "great escape"?

#6 In 2012 Lionel Messi scored a record number of goals in competitive matches for club and country. Was it 81, 91, or 101?

#7 In which country did Roy Hodgson start his managerial career?

#8 Who said, "I would not be bothered if we lost every game as long as we won the league"?
Jonathan Woodgate or Mark Viduka?

#9 Which country's state investment fund bought Paris Saint-Germain in 2011?

#10 Who scored Man United's two late goals, when they beat Bayern Munich in the 1999 Champions League final?

ANSWERS ON PAGE 85

WORD SEARCH #5:
World Cup Finalists

```
O Q K B R A Z I L K Q H X D S
N V S F S D N A L R E H T E N
B Y Z E V N Y N P E N Q Y C W
K F Q N I X E D I P U Q N N X
I A T A A F V Z E Z U D Y A A
M K P I A B G W L L M N Y R N
N S E N G L A N D J A R C F I
S E H Y W I U U Q M V N Q B T
I P D G R I K J R V V R V A N
W X R E H A J E E G T W I I E
L D F T W Y G Z K U N T B V G
W Q B E B S L N Z W A D U S R
Y A U G U R U B U O M A K R A
G C I L B U P E R H C E Z C E
O I T A L Y P C P S U J R U U
```

Brazil, Germany, Italy, Argentina, France, Uruguay, England, Spain, Netherlands, Hungary, Czech Republic, Sweden, Croatia

ANSWERS ON PAGE 82

ON THE MAP:
South America at the World Cup Finals

Can you name the seven South American countries that have reached at least the Quarter Finals of the World Cup?

One point for each country, another point for each of the seven that you identify correctly on the map opposite.

#1 _____

#2 _____

#3 _____

#4 _____

#5 _____

#6 _____

#7 _____

ANSWERS ON PAGE 83

QUIZ 7:
A Potential Banana Skin

#1 Which club did Jürgen Klopp start his managerial career with?

#2 Who said, "I can see the carrot at the end of the tunnel"?
Sol Campbell or Stuart Pearce?

#3 In which country was the 1982 World Cup played?

#4 Louis Saha scored after just 25 seconds of the 2009 FA Cup Final, but who was he playing for at the time?

#5 Which English club was the first to hold both the Europa League and Champions League trophies at the same time?

#6 One highlight of Leicester City's 2015/16 title winning season was Jamie Vardy's run of goals in 2015. How many consecutive matches did he score in?

#7 Alex Ferguson won the European Cup Winners' Cup with two different clubs. Can you name them?

#8 Who said, "I couldn't settle in Italy. It was like living in a foreign country"?
Danny Dichio or Ian Rush?

#9 Which Sunderland striker won the Golden Boot in the 1999/2000 Premier League season?

#10 Which Man United player was the first to be sent off in an FA Cup Final?

ANSWERS ON PAGE 89

CRYPTOGRAMS: Grounds

Can you work out which letters correspond to which numbers, and find the names of four football stadiums? Start by guessing some of the common letters, or even a full stadium name.

A	B	C	D	E	F	G	H	I	J	K	L	M

N	O	P	Q	R	S	T	U	V	W	X	Y	Z
14	18				19	5						

_ _ O T _ _ N _
19 26 18 5 1 20 14 25

_ _ _ _ _ _   _ T _ _ _ _
9 20 1 23 24 11   19 5 20 25 2 6 23

_ O _ T _ _ N   _ O _ _
26 18 11 5 23 20 14   11 18 20 25

_ _ _ N   _ O _ _ T
25 24 20 14   3 18 6 11 5

ANSWERS ON PAGE 75

WHO AM I #4?

#1 I was born in Leytonstone, on 2nd May 1975.

#2 I made my league debut while on loan at Preston North End.

#3 I was the first England player to be sent off twice.

#4 I won the Goal of the Decade award at the Premier League 10 Seasons Awards.

who am I? _____

ANSWER AT THE BOTTOM OF THE NEXT PAGE

43

BEAT THE CLOCK:
England in the 90s

Thirty-three players made their England debuts in the 1990s. You have five minutes, how many of them can you name?

ANSWERS ON PAGE 81

Who Am I #4? David Beckham

ANAGRAMS:

Premier League Players

#1   Reel Nightmares   _____

#2   Oh Mama Lashed   _____

#3   Ferns Array   _____

#4   Saucing Led   _____

#5   Icier Red   _____

#6   Army Bath Mama   _____

#7   Bill El Wench   _____

#8   Jam Zine Rule   _____

#9   A Taxing Hark   _____

#10   Litany Marathon   _____

ANSWERS ON PAGE 70

NAME THE TEAM:
Real Madrid - La Decima

Real Madrid made history by winning a tenth European Cup/Champions League in 2014. Below are the starting eleven's initials. Write down the full names on the page opposite.

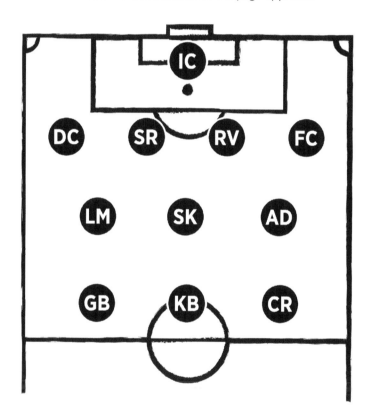

#1 **IC** _____

#2 **DC** _____

#3 **SR** _____

#4 **RV** _____

#5 **FC** _____

#6 **LM** _____

#7 **SK** _____

#8 **AD** _____

#9 **GB** _____

#10 **KB** _____

#11 **CR** _____

ANSWERS ON PAGE 88

MATCH UP:
Match the Team with the Stadium

#1	Wigan Athletic	Vicarage Road
#2	Bradford City	The Den
#3	Reading	Kirklees Stadium
#4	Huddersfield Town	Madejski Stadium
#5	Preston North End	Fratton Park
#6	Barnsley	Turf Moor
#7	Watford	Deepdale
#8	Burnley	DW Stadium
#9	Portsmouth	Oakwell
#10	Millwall	Valley Parade

ANSWERS ON PAGE 87

QUIZ 8:
The Ref's Word is Final

#1 Which team won the first FA Women's Super League in 2011?

#2 Tommy Hutchinson scored two goals in the 1981 FA Cup Final - what was unusual about this achievement?

#3 Lionel Messi and Christiano Ronaldo have both scored over 100 Champions League goals. Which of them reached the target first?

#4 Who said, "If you closed your eyes, you couldn't tell the difference between the two sides"?
Neil Warnock or Phil Brown?

#5 Bayern Munich beat which Portuguese team 12-1 on aggregate, in the 2008/9 Champions League round of 16?

#6 How old was Kylian Mbappé when he won the World Cup with France?

#7 Who said, "My biggest mentor is myself because I've had to study and that's been my biggest influence"? Alan Pardew or Brendan Rodgers?

#8 Can you name the only Premier League goalkeeper to reach 200 clean sheets?

#9 In 2001, Gareth Morris scored an FA Cup goal within the first ten seconds of the match. How many seconds were on the clock when he scored?

#10 How many league titles did Everton win in the 1980s?

ANSWERS ON PAGE 92

ANSWERS

QUIZ 1
Early Doors

#1 Who said, "I'm going to make a prediction - it could go either way"? John Motson or Ron Atkinson?
Ron Atkinson

#2 Who was the top scorer at the 2014 World Cup finals? Thomas Muller, Karim Banzema or James Rodriguez?
James Rodriguez scored 6 goals for Colombia.

#3 Who won the first FA Cup Final in 1872? Royal Engineers, Wanderers, or Old Etonians?
Wanderers. Based in London, they have no link to Wolves or Bolton.

#4 Which goalkeeper has played over 150 times in the Champions League?
Iker Casillas. He played 150 games for Real Madrid, before continuing his Champions League adventure at Porto.

#5 Marta is considered one of the best female footballers of all time. Which country did she play for?
Brazil.

#6 The English Football League Cup has had many names over the years, but which of these names is made up? Rumbelows Cup, Worthington Cup, or Nationwide Cup?
Nationwide Cup. Nationwide sponsored the football league, but not the cup.

#7 Who was the top scorer in the very first Premier League season? Teddy Sheringham, Andy Cole, or Alan Shearer?
Teddy Sheringham.

#8 Which team did Luis Suarez play for before Liverpool?
Ajax.

#9 When were goalkeepers first allowed in football? 1861, 1871 or 1881?
1871.

#10 In which country do the team Newell's Old Boys play?
Argentina.

BEAT THE CLOCK
The Start of the Premier League

#1   Arsenal

#2   Aston Villa

#3   Blackburn Rovers

#4   Chelsea

#5   Coventry City

#6   Crystal Palace

#7   Everton

#8   Ipswich Town

#9   Leeds United

#10   Liverpool

#11   Manchester City

#12   Manchester United

#13   Middlesbrough

#14   Norwich City

#15   Nottingham Forest

#16   Oldham Athletic

#17   Queens Park Rangers

#18   Sheffield United

#19   Sheffield Wednesday

#20   Southampton

#21   Tottenham Hotspur

#22   Wimbledon

ON THE MAP
European Cup Winners

#1	Celtic	#12	Bayern Munich
#2	Manchester United	#13	Marseille
#3	Liverpool	#14	Real Madrid
#4	Nottingham Forest	#15	Barcelona
#5	Aston Villa	#16	Porto
#6	Chelsea	#17	Benfica
#7	Ajax	#18	Juventus
#8	Feyenoord	#19	AC Milan
#9	PSV Eindhoven	#20	Internazionale
#10	Borussia Dortmund	#21	Red Star Belgrade
#11	Hamburger SV	#22	Steaua Bucharest

QUIZ 2
Over the Moon

#1 Who said, "If we played like this every week, we wouldn't be so inconsistent"? Paul Gascoigne or Bryan Robson?
Bryan Robson.

#2 Which two teams played in the 1974 World Cup Final, and for a bonus what was the score?
West Germany beat Netherlands (Holland) by two goals to one.

#3 Which of these grounds has the FA Cup Final NOT been played at? Kennington Oval, Anfield or Old Trafford?
Anfield.

#4 Which country's teams have won the European Cup/Champions League the most times?
Spain.

#5 Who won the first women's Ballon d'Or? Carly Lloyd, Lucy Bronze or Ada Hegerberg?
Ada Hegerberg.

#6 Who won the very first EFL Cup? Birmingham City, Aston Villa, or Chelsea?
Aston Villa beat Rotherham United in 1961.

#7 Eleven of the first twelve Premier League titles were shared between Man United and Arsenal. Who won the other one?
Blackburn in 1994/5.

#8 Which country does Robert Lewandowski represent at international level?
Poland.

#9 In what year was the back-pass rule introduced? 1992, 1994 or 1995?
1992.

#10 In which country do Club Necaxa play?
Mexico.

WORD SEARCH #1
Find the Top Premier League Scorers

```
.  .  V  A  N  P  E  R  S  I  E  .  M  .  .
.  .  D  Y  .  .  .  .  .  .  .  A  .  R  .
.  .  N  R  .  .  .  .  .  H  .  .  E  .
.  .  A  N  .  .  .  .  G  .  N  .  R  .
.  .  N  E  .  .  .  .  N  .  .  E  .  A  .
.  .  I  H  .  .  D  I  .  .  .  W  .  E  .
.  .  D  .  .  .  R  R  .  .  .  O  .  H  .
.  .  R  .  .  E  E  R  A  .  .  .  .  S  .
.  .  E  .  H  .  O  O  .  P  .  .  .  .  O
.  .  F  S  .  .  F  O  F  .  M  .  .  R  .
E  .  .  .  .  .  E  N  O  .  .  A  E  .  .
.  N  E  L  O  C  D  E  W  .  .  U  L  .  .
.  .  A  .  .  .  .  Y  L  .  G  .  .  .  .
.  .  .  K  .  .  .  .  E  A  .  .  .  .  .
.  .  .  .  .  .  .  .  R  .  .  .  .  .  .
```

Cole, Kane, Owen, Defoe, Henry, Aguero, Fowler, Rooney,
Lampard, Shearer, Ferdinand, VanPersie, Sheringham

ANAGRAMS
English League Teams

#1   A HEM UNTWISTED   West Ham United

#2   TWINS NOD NOW   Swindon Town

#3   A INTERESTED MUNCH   Manchester United

#4   HOP TO THE TANTRUMS   Tottenham Hotspur

#5   HONEST FORMATTING   Nottingham Forest

#6   APT LOVER   Port Vale

#7   TEN OVER   Everton

#8   OUT PHANTOMS   Southampton

#9   RAVENS CORK BLURB   Blackburn Rovers

#10 I DELUDE NEST   Leeds United

QUIZ 3
Park the Bus

#1 Which country won the very first World Cup?
Uruguay, in 1930.

#2 Who were the first Welsh team to win the FA Cup?
Cardiff. They beat Arsenal 1-0 in 1927.

#3 During the 1970s two teams won the European Cup three years in a row. Can you name them?
Ajax (1970-72) and Bayern Munich (1973-75).

#4 Which World Cup winner scored 49 goals in EFL Cup games? Geoff Hurst, Bobby Charlton or Martin Peters?
Geoff Hurst.

#5 Who said, "Not to win is guttering"? Andy Carroll or Mark Noble?
Mark Noble.

#6 Pele only played for two club teams during his career. One was Santos in Brazil. Can you name the other?
New York Cosmos.

#7 What does VAR stand for?
Video Assistant Referee.

#8 In which country do the team Hadjuk Split play?
Croatia.

#9 In 2015 John Carver managed which Premier League club for twenty games?
Newcastle United.

#10 Who said, "If history repeats itself, I should think we can expect the same thing again"? Kevin Keegan or Terry Venables?
Terry Venables.

MISSING LETTERS
English League Teams

#1   Ipswich Town

#2   Blackpool

#3   Bradford City

#4   Watford

#5   Chelsea

#6   Milton Keynes Dons

#7   Leicester City

#8   Bristol City

#9   Preston North End

#10   Arsenal

MISSING LETTERS
Players

#1   Harry Kane

#2   Ismaïla Sarr

#3   Kevin De Bruyne

#4   Victor Lindelöf

#5   Callum Wilson

#6   Michael Keane

#7   Ross Barkley

#8   Bernd Leno

#9   Sadio Mané

#10   Ricardo Pereira

QUIZ 4
A Game of Two Halves

#1 Italy won their first World title in 1934. Where was the match played, Rome or Paris?
Rome. They also won the 1938 World Cup in Paris.

#2 Which team has won the European Cup more times than they've won their own domestic league?
Nottingham Forest. They won the English title just the once, but the European Cup twice (qualifying the second time as holders).

#3 Who said, "The first ninety minutes of a football match are the most important"? Pep Guardiola or Bobby Robson?
Bobby Robson.

#4 England's women reached the semi-finals in both the 2015 and 2019 World Cups. Which teams knocked them out?
Japan in 2015. USA in 2019. Both games ended 2-1.

#5 Who were the first team to be relegated from the Premier League twice? Crystal Palace, Middlesbrough, or Nottingham Forest?
Crystal Palace were relegated in 1993, came back up in 1994, and then went back down again in 1995.

#6 Maradona's international career ended in the middle of the 1994 World Cup finals. What was the reason?
He failed a drug test and had to leave the tournament early.

#7 Which was formed first, FIFA or UEFA?
FIFA. FIFA was formed in 1904, UEFA in 1954.

#8 Al Ahly are by far the most successful football team in which country?
Egypt.

#9 Which Portuguese club did José Mourinho first manage?
Benfica. He left after less than a dozen games, and went on to manage União de Leiria, and then Porto.

#10 Who said, "Germany are a very difficult team to play...they had 11 internationals out there today"? Neil Lennon or Steve Lomas?
Steve Lomas.

ANAGRAMS
English League Grounds

#1 Big Mod Drafters   Stamford Bridge

#2 Country Dig   City Ground

#3 Die Like Muskrats   Kirklees Stadium

#4 Dismays At Strum   St Mary's Stadium

#5 Doors A Poking   Goodison Park

#6 Fine Lad   Anfield

#7 Hi Flutist Dogma   Stadium of Light

#8 Loaned Lard   Elland Road

#9 Mu Ex Lion   Molineux

#10 No Stupid Wigmaker   King Power Stadium

NAME THE TEAM
England World Cup 2018 Semi-Finalists

#1 **JP** Jordan Pickford

#2 **KW** Kyle Walker

#3 **JS** John Stones

#4 **HM** Harry Maguire

#5 **DA** Dele Alli

#6 **JH** Jordan Henderson

#7 **JL** Jesse Lingard

#8 **KT** Kieran Trippier

#9 **AY** Ashley Young

#10 **HK** Harry Kane

#11 **RS** Raheem Sterling

WORD SEARCH #2
Players

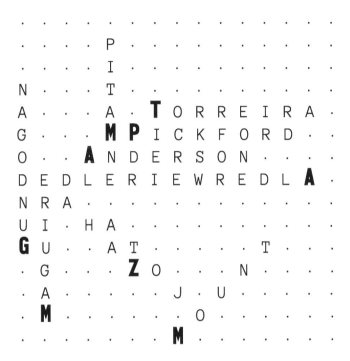

```
.   .   .   .   .   .   .   .   .   .   .   .   .
.   .   .   .   P   .   .   .   .   .   .   .   .
.   .   .   .   I   .   .   .   .   .   .   .   .
N   .   .   .   T   .   .   .   .   .   .   .   .
A   .   .   .   A   .   T   O   R   R   E   I   R   A   .
G   .   .   .   M   P   I   C   K   F   O   R   D   .   .
O   .   .   A   N   D   E   R   S   O   N   .   .   .   .
D   E   D   L   E   R   I   E   W   R   E   D   L   A   .
N   R   A   .   .   .   .   .   .   .   .   .   .   .
U   I   .   H   A   .   .   .   .   .   .   .   .   .
G   U   .   A   T   .   .   .   .   T   .   .   .
.   G   .   .   Z   O   .   .   N   .   .   .   .
.   A   .   .   .   .   J   .   U   .   .   .   .
.   M   .   .   .   .   .   O   .   .   .   .   .
.   .   .   .   .   .   M   .   .   .   .   .   .
```

ZAHA, MATIP, MOUNT, MAGUIRE, ANDERSON, GUNDOGAN, PICKFORD, TORREIRA, ALDERWEIRELD

ANAGRAMS
Premier League Players

#	Anagram	Player
#1	Reel Nightmares	Raheem Sterling
#2	Oh Mama Lashed	Mohamed Salah
#3	Ferns Array	Ryan Fraser
#4	Saucing Led	Lucas Digne
#5	Icier Red	Eric Dier
#6	Army Bath Mama	Tammy Abraham
#7	Bill El Wench	Ben Chilwell
#8	Jam Zine Rule	Raúl Jiménez
#9	A Taxing Hark	Granit Xhaka
#10	Litany Marathon	Anthony Martial

WORD SEARCH #3
Grounds

```
·  H  G  U  O  R  O  B  S  L  L  I  H  ·  ·
·  ·  C  R  A  V  E  N  C  O  T  T  A  G  E
·  ·  K  R  A  P  S  E  M  A  J  T  S  ·  ·
S  N  R  O  H  T  W  A  H  E  H  T  Y  ·  ·
·  ·  ·  ·  ·  ·  ·  ·  K  ·  ·  E  ·  ·  ·
·  ·  ·  ·  ·  ·  ·  R  ·  ·  L  ·  ·  ·  ·
·  ·  ·  ·  ·  ·  A  ·  ·  L  ·  ·  ·  ·  ·
·  ·  ·  ·  ·  P  ·  ·  A  ·  ·  ·  ·  ·  ·
·  ·  ·  A  ·  ·  V  ·  ·  ·  ·  ·  ·  ·  ·
·  ·  ·  L  ·  ·  E  ·  ·  ·  ·  ·  ·  ·  ·
·  ·  L  ·  ·  H  ·  ·  ·  ·  ·  ·  ·  ·  ·
·  I  ·  ·  T  ·  K  R  A  P  E  D  I  R  P
V  ·  ·  ·  ·  ·  E  D  I  S  R  E  V  I  R
·  E  N  A  L  L  A  M  A  R  B  ·  ·  ·
·  ·  D  A  O  R  S  U  T  F  O  L  ·  ·  ·
```

St James Park, Bramall Lane, Villa Park, The Valley, Hillsborough, Riverside, Pride Park, The Hawthorns, Craven Cottage, Loftus Road

QUIZ 5
A Six Pointer

#1 In 2016 Derby County beat Carlisle United after a
monumental penalty shootout. How many penalties
were taken? 26, 29, or 32?
*32. The final result was 14-13 to Derby - the rest were
missed.*

#2 England beat West Germany in the 1966 World Cup.
Geoff Hurst famously scored a hat-trick, but who
scored England's other goal?
Martin Peters.

#3 Man City scored six goals against Watford in the 2019
FA Cup Final. Which team had previously scored six in
a final?
Bury, against Derby County in 1903.

#4 Celtic reached the final of the 1970 European Cup, but
what was unusual about their second round tie with
Benfica in that year's competition?
*The tie ended up 3-3 on aggregate and was decided
with the toss of a coin - the last time this happened in
the European Cup.*

#5 Between 2016 and 2019, this French team won the Women's Champions League every season. Can you name that club?
Lyon (Olympique Lyonnais).

#6 Which team won the final First Division title, prior to the start of the Premier League?
Leeds United.

#7 Who said, "We must have had 99 per cent of the match. It was the other three per cent that cost us"? Gianluca Vialli or Ruud Gullit?
Ruud Gullit.

#8 Man United and Man City famously tied on points in the 2011/12 season, with Man City winning the title on goal difference. How many points did they tie on?
89.

#9 Between 2008 and 2017, Messi and Ronaldo were the only winners of the Ballon D'or. Can you name the Brazilian who won in 2007, and the player who ended their dominance in 2018?
Kaká won in 2007, and Luka Modrić won in 2018.

#10 Which of these teams has Sam Allardyce not managed? Sunderland, Everton, Portsmouth, or Blackburn Rovers?
Portsmouth.

NAME THE OPPOSITION
England Games

Germany   **1 v 5**   **England**

Owen 12, 48, 65
Gerrard 45+4
Heskey 73'

Spain   **2 v 3**   **England**

Sterling 1', 38
Rashford 30

England   **2 v 2**   **Argentina**

Shearer 9
Owen 16

England   **3 v 2**   **Cameroon**

Platt 25
Lineker 83 (pen.), 105 (pen.)

CRYPTOGRAMS
Grounds

A	B	C	D	E	F	G	H	I	J	K	L	M
20		3	25	24	9			2			1	23

N	O	P	Q	R	S	T	U	V	W	X	Y	Z
14	18	26		11	19	5	6					

S P O T L A N D
19 26 18 5 1 20 14 25

F A L M E R   S T A D I U M
9 20 1 23 24 11   19 5 20 25 2 6 23

P O R T M A N   R O A D
26 18 11 5 23 20 14   11 18 20 25

D E A N   C O U R T
25 24 20 14   3 18 6 11 5

WORD SEARCH #4
Teams

```
·  S  U  N  D  E  R  L  A  N  D  ·  ·  D  M
·  ·  ·  ·  ·  ·  ·  ·  ·  ·  ·  ·  E  A
M  A  S  T  O  N  V  I  L  L  A  ·  ·  T  N
N  I  ·  ·  ·  ·  ·  ·  ·  L  ·  ·  I  C
O  Y  D  ·  Y  T  I  C  E  K  O  T  S  N  H
T  ·  T  D  ·  ·  ·  ·  ·  ·  O  ·  ·  U  E
H  ·  ·  N  L  ·  ·  ·  ·  ·  P  ·  ·  E  S
G  ·  ·  ·  U  E  ·  ·  ·  ·  R  ·  ·  L  T
I  ·  ·  ·  O  S  ·  ·  ·  E  ·  ·  T  E
R  ·  ·  S  ·  ·  C  B  ·  ·  V  ·  ·  S  R
B  ·  ·  E  ·  ·  ·  Y  R  ·  I  ·  ·  A  C
·  ·  ·  V  ·  ·  ·  ·  B  O  L  ·  ·  C  I
·  ·  ·  L  ·  ·  ·  ·  ·  R  U  ·  ·  W  T
·  ·  ·  O  ·  ·  ·  ·  ·  ·  E  G  ·  E  Y
·  ·  ·  W  ·  ·  ·  ·  ·  ·  D  H  N  ·
```

Wolves, Newcastle United, Stoke City, Aston Villa, Middlesbrough, Sunderland, Derby County, Manchester City, Liverpool, Brighton

BEAT THE CLOCK
All the Uniteds and Cities

Birmingham City

Bradford City

Bristol City

Cambridge United

Cardiff City

Carlisle United

Colchester United

Coventry City

Exeter City

Hull City

Leeds United

Leicester City

Lincoln City

Manchester City

Manchester United

Newcastle United

Norwich City

Oxford United

Peterborough United

Rotherham United

Salford City

Scunthorpe United

Sheffield United

Southend United

Stoke City

Swansea City

West Ham United

NAME THE TEAM
Arsenal 2003/4 - The Invincibles

#1   **JL**   Jens Lehmann

#2   **L**   Lauren

#3   **KT**   Kolo Touré

#4   **SC**   Sol Campbell

#5   **AC**   Ashley Cole

#6   **FL**   Frederick Ljungberg

#7   **PV**   Patrick Vieira

#8   **GS**   Gilberto Silva

#9   **RP**   Robert Pirès*

#10   **DB**   Dennis Bergkamp

#11   **TH**   Thierry Henry

*Ray Parlour was also a squad member this season, but played fewer games than Robert Pirès (or any of the above players).

MATCH UP
Where did they make their debuts?

#1	Nathan Aké	Chelsea
#2	Joelinton	Sport Recife
#3	Felipe Anderson	Santos
#4	Dele Alli	MK Dons
#5	Bernardo Silva	Benfica B
#6	James Maddison	Coventry City
#7	Rúben Neves	Porto
#8	Alisson	Internacional
#9	Eric Dier	Sporting Lisbon B
#10	Jordan Pickford	Darlington

NAME THE OPPOSITION
FA Cup Finals

Arsenal   **2 v 1**   **Chelsea**
Sánchez 4
Ramsey 79

Portsmouth   **1 v 0**   **Cardiff City**
Kanu 37

Wigan Athletic   **1 v 0**   **Man City**
Watson 90+1

Wimbledon   **1 v 0**   **Liverpool**
Sanchez 37

BEAT THE CLOCK
England in the 90s

Gareth Barry	Ledley King	Robert Green
Steven Gerrard	Jermaine Jenas	Peter Crouch
Ashley Cole	Paul Robinson	Darren Bent
Alan Smith	Wayne Rooney	Theo Walcott
Danny Mills	Matthew Upson	Aaron Lennon
Michael Carrick	John Terry	Micah Richards
Joe Cole	Scott Parker	Joleon Lescott
Owen Hargreaves	Glen Johnson	Ashley Young
Trevor Sinclair	Jermain Defoe	Phil Jagielka
Darius Vassell	Shaun Wright-Phillips	Joe Hart
Wayne Bridge	Stewart Downing	James Milner

WORD SEARCH #5
World Cup Finalists

```
.  .  .  B  R  A  Z  I  L  .  .  .  .  .  .
.  .  .  .  S  D  N  A  L  R  E  H  T  E  N
.  .  .  .  .  N  .  .  .  .  .  .  C  .
.  .  .  .  I  .  .  .  .  .  .  N  .
.  .  .  A  .  .  .  .  .  .  Y  A  A  .
.  .  P  .  .  .  .  .  .  N  .  R  N
N  S  E  N  G  L  A  N  D  .  A  .  .  F  I
.  E  .  Y  .  .  .  .  M  .  .  .  .  T
.  .  D  .  R  .  .  R  .  .  .  A  N
.  .  .  E  .  A  .  E  .  .  .  .  I  E
.  .  .  .  W  .  G  .  .  .  .  T  .  G
.  .  .  .  .  S  .  N  .  .  A  .  .  R
Y  A  U  G  U  R  U  .  U  O  .  .  .  .  A
.  C  I  L  B  U  P  E  R  H  C  E  Z  C  .
.  I  T  A  L  Y  .  C  .  .  .  .  .  .  .
```

Brazil, Germany, Italy, Argentina, France, Uruguay, England, Spain, Netherlands, Hungary, Czech Republic, Sweden, Croatia

ON THE MAP
South America at the World Cup Finals

#1   Colombia

#2   Peru

#3   Argentina

#4   Chile

#5   Brazil

#6   Uruguay

#7   Paraguay

CRYPTOGRAMS
Premier League Players

A	B	C	D	E	F	G	H	I	J	K	L	M
9			15	13	18	1	12	5	2		20	17

N	O	P	Q	R	S	T	U	V	W	X	Y	Z
8	26	21		25	7	16	19		10			22

```
  D   I   O   G   O        J   O   T   A
  15  5   26  1   26       2   26  16  9

W   I   L   F   R   I   E   D       Z   A   H   A
10  5   20  18  25  5   13  15      22  9   12  9

  M   A   S   O   N        M   O   U   N   T
  17  9   7   26  8        17  26  19  8   16

  J   O   E   L        M   A   T   I   P
  2   26  13  20       17  9   16  5   21
```

QUIZ 6
Give it 110%

#1 Who said, "He dribbles a lot and the opposition don't like it - you can see it all over their faces"? Kevin Keegan or Ron Atkinson?
Ron Atkinson.

#2 Roger Milla was 42 when he played in the 1994 World Cup finals. Which country did he play for?
Cameroon.

#3 Ashley Cole won the FA Cup more times than any other player. How many winners' medals does he have?
Seven. He won it three times with Arsenal, and four with Chelsea.

#4 Liverpool came from three down at half time to beat which team in the 2005 Champions League final?
They beat Milan.

#5 In the 2004/5 Premier League season, the team which were bottom at Christmas managed to avoid relegation on the final day. Which club performed this "great escape"?
West Bromwich Albion.

#6 In 2012 Lionel Messi scored a record number of goals in competitive matches for club and country. Was it 81, 91, or 101?

He scored an astonishing 91 goals in 2012 (and five more in friendlies, just for good measure!)

#7 In which country did Roy Hodgson start his managerial career?

Sweden. He became manager of Halmstad in 1976.

#8 Who said, "I would not be bothered if we lost every game as long as we won the league"? Jonathan Woodgate or Mark Viduka?

Mark Viduka.

#9 Which country's state investment fund bought Paris Saint-Germain in 2011?

Qatar.

#10 Who scored Man United's two late goals, when they beat Bayern Munich in the 1999 Champions League final?

Teddy Sheringham and Ole Gunnar Solskjær.

MATCH UP
Match the Team with the Stadium

#1	Wigan Athletic	DW Stadium
#2	Bradford City	Valley Parade
#3	Reading	Madejski Stadium
#4	Huddersfield Town	Kirklees Stadium
#5	Preston North End	Deepdale
#6	Barnsley	Oakwell
#7	Watford	Vicarage Road
#8	Burnley	Turf Moor
#9	Portsmouth	Fratton Park
#10	Millwall	The Den

NAME THE TEAM
Real Madrid - La Decima

#1   **IC**   Iker Casillas

#2   **DC**   Dani Carvajal

#3   **SR**   Sergio Ramos

#4   **RV**   Raphaël Varane

#5   **FC**   Fábio Coentrão

#6   **LM**   Luka Modrić

#7   **SK**   Sami Khedira

#8   **AD**   Ángel Di María

#9   **GB**   Gareth Bale

#10   **KB**   Karim Benzema

#11   **CR**   Cristiano Ronaldo

QUIZ 7
A Potential Banana Skin

#1 Which club did Jürgen Klopp start his managerial career with?
Mainz 05.

#2 Who said, "I can see the carrot at the end of the tunnel"? Sol Campbell or Stuart Pearce?
Stuart Pearce.

#3 In which country was the 1982 World Cup played?
It was played in Spain. Italy beat West Germany in the final.

#4 Louis Saha scored after just 25 seconds of the 2009 FA Cup Final, but who was he playing for at the time?
Everton. They eventually lost the match 2-1 to Chelsea.

#5 Which English club was the first to hold both the Europa League and Champions League trophies at the same time?
Chelsea - they won the Champions League in 2012, and then the Europa League in 2013, the final taking place before that season's Champions League final.

#6 One highlight of Leicester City's 2015/16 title winning season was Jamie Vardy's run of goals in 2015. How many consecutive matches did he score in?
Eleven - between 29th August and 28th November.

#7 Alex Ferguson won the European Cup Winners' Cup with two different clubs. Can you name them?
Aberdeen and Manchester United.

#8 Who said, "I couldn't settle in Italy. It was like living in a foreign country"? Danny Dichio or Ian Rush?
Ian Rush.

#9 Which Sunderland striker won the Golden Boot in the 1999/2000 Premier League season?
Kevin Phillips.

#10 Which Man United player was the first to be sent off in an FA Cup Final?
Kevin Moran, for a foul on Peter Reid of Everton, in the 1985 final. United still won the match.

MATCH UP
Match the Player with the Country

#	Player		Country
#1	Alireza Jahanbakhsh		Iran
#2	Seamus Coleman		Ireland
#3	Sead Kolasinac		Bosnia-Herzegovina
#4	Michael Hector		Jamaica
#5	Joel Matip		Cameroon
#6	Granit Xhaka		Switzerland
#7	Andrew Robertson		Scotland
#8	Nicolas Pépé		Cote d'Ivoire
#9	Rodri		Spain
#10	N'Golo Kanté		France

QUIZ 8
The Ref's Word is Final

#1 Which team won the first FA Women's Super League in 2011?
Arsenal.

#2 Tommy Hutchinson scored two goals in the 1981 FA Cup Final - what was unusual about this achievement?
He scored for his own team Man City, then in the 79th minute, he deflected a Spurs free kick into his own goal - levelling the match. Spurs won the replay 3-2.

#3 Lionel Messi and Christiano Ronaldo have both scored over 100 Champions League goals. Which of them reached the target first?
Ronaldo was the first to reach 100.

#4 Who said, "If you closed your eyes, you couldn't tell the difference between the two sides"? Neil Warnock or Phil Brown?
Phil Brown.

#5 Bayern Munich beat which Portuguese team 12-1 on aggregate, in the 2008/9 Champions League round of 16?
Sporting CP (or Sporting Lisbon).

#6 How old was Kylian Mbappé when he won the World Cup with France?
19.

#7 Who said, "My biggest mentor is myself because I've had to study and that's been my biggest influence"? Alan Pardew or Brendan Rodgers?
Brendan Rodgers.

#8 Can you name the only Premier League goalkeeper to reach 200 clean sheets?
Petr Čech.

#9 In 2001, Gareth Morris scored an FA Cup goal within the first ten seconds of the match. How many seconds were on the clock when he scored?
Astonishingly, just four seconds! Gareth was playing for Ashton United against Skelmersdale United.

#10 How many league titles did Everton win in the 1980s?
Two, in 1984/85, and 1986/87.

Thanks for playing

We hope you enjoyed the book, and look forward to sharing more great quizzes and puzzles with you.

CREATED BY FANS FOR FANS can be contacted at
createdbyfansforfans@gmail.com

Printed by Amazon Italia Logistica S.r.l.
Torrazza Piemonte (TO), Italy

11958652R00059